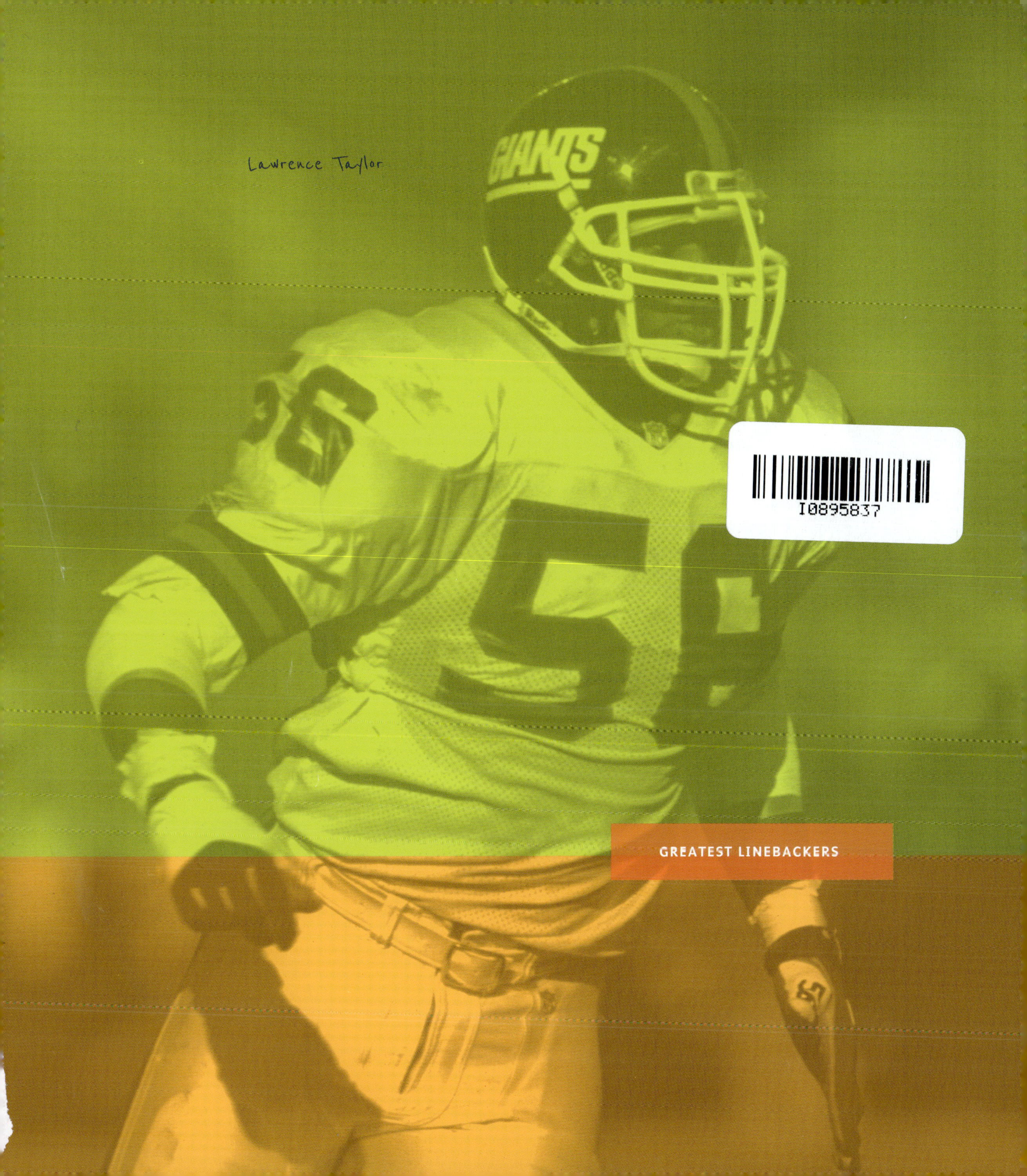
Lawrence Taylor

GREATEST LINEBACKERS

Dick Butkus

NFL HALL OF FAMERS

GREATEST LINEBACKERS

JOE TISCHLER

Jack Ham

CREATIVE SPORTS

CREATIVE EDUCATION / CREATIVE PAPERBACKS

Published by Creative Education and Creative Paperbacks
P.O. Box 227, Mankato, Minnesota 56002
Creative Education and Creative Paperbacks
are imprints of The Creative Company
www.thecreativecompany.us

Design and production by Blue Design (www.bluedes.com)
Art direction by Rita Marshall

Images by Associated Press/Four Seam Images, 1; Getty Images/Al Messerschmidt, 4–5, 32, Bill Eppridge/Time Life Pictures, 7, Focus On Sport, cover, 2, 6, 7, 9, 14, 15, 21, G Fiume, 30, George Gojkovich, 3, 12, 17, 19, Gregory Shamus, 7, Kidwiler Collection, 7, Michael Zagaris, 6, New York Daily News Archive, 11, NFL/Pro Football Hall of Fame, 6, Owen C. Shaw, 25, Ron Vesely, 26, Sporting News Archive, 10, TIMOTHY A. CLARY, 6; NFL/Don Lansu/WireImage.com, 22, Manny Rubio/WireImage.com, 18, Michael Montes, 29; Wikimedia Commons/Gonzo fan2007, cover (background), Photographer's Mate 3rd Class Ben Gonzales , USN, 28

Library of Congress Cataloging-in-Publication Data
Names: Tischler, Joe, author.
Title: Greatest linebackers / Joe Tischler.
Description: Mankato, Minnesota : Creative Education and Creative Paperbacks, [2026] | Series: Creative sports: NFL hall of famers | Includes index. | Audience: Ages 8–12 | Audience: Grades 4–6 | Summary: "Photo-driven and stat-filled, this middle-grade NFL title showcases 11 of pro football's greatest linebackers enshrined in the Hall of Fame, from Chuck Bednarik and Dick Butkus to Mike Singletary and Ray Lewis"—Provided by publisher.
Identifiers: LCCN 2024048103 (print) | LCCN 2024048104 (ebook) | ISBN 9798889896142 (library binding) | ISBN 9781682777800 (paperback) | ISBN 9798889896944 (ebook)
Subjects: LCSH: Linebackers (Football)—Biography—Juvenile literature. | Football players—Biography—Juvenile literature. | Pro Football Hall of Fame (U.S.)—Juvenile literature.
Classification: LCC GV939.A1 T56 2026 (print) | LCC GV939.A1 (ebook) | DDC 796.332092/2 [B]—dc23/eng/20241202
LC record available at https://lccn.loc.gov/2024048103
LC ebook record available at https://lccn.loc.gov/2024048104

Printed in India

Ray Lewis

60

MOSS
81
ny

TAYLOR
56

42
42

CONTENTS

TIMEOUT

INTRODUCTION

At the snap, linebacker Lawrence Taylor charged like a cheetah. His goal? Sack the quarterback. And sack he did, for a career total of 132.5!

Like all players in his position, Taylor's job was to keep the opposing team's offense out of the end zone. That might mean sacking the quarterback. It might mean tackling the running back or making an interception. Football linebackers are rock solid. They combine strength, skill, and attitude. All linebackers who play for the National Football League (NFL) are at the top of their game. But only a handful can be called Hall of Famers.

The Pro Football Hall of Fame honors 378 past players, coaches, and sport contributors. Of those, 38 are linebackers. This book highlights 11 linebackers. This list isn't a ranking. Players are ordered by the year they were enshrined. Of the 11 Hall of Fame linebackers featured here, 8 are Super Bowl champions.

Lawrence Taylor

CHUCK BEDNARIK (1925–2015)
LINEBACKER/CENTER
PHILADELPHIA EAGLES SEASONS: 1949–62
HALL OF FAME CLASS: 1967
AWARDS/HONORS: MEMBER OF NFL 50TH/75TH/100TH ANNIVERSARY TEAMS, 8X PRO BOWL, 9X ALL-PRO (6X FIRST TEAM), 2X NFL CHAMPION

CHUCK BEDNARIK

One player who lived and breathed the city of Philadelphia, Pennsylvania, was Chuck Bednarik. Bednarik was born just north of the city, in Bethlehem. He went to college in Philly at the University of Pennsylvania. In the 1949 NFL Draft, he was the number one pick of the Eagles. Before his football careers, Bednarik served in the U.S. Air Force. He flew 30 combat missions over Nazi Germany during World War II (1939–45).

When Bednarik returned from the war, his focus was football. In college, he played both center on offense and linebacker on defense. These positions are known for their physical play. He continued to play both positions once he went pro with the Eagles. He is known as one of the NFL's last "two-way" players. Bednarik earned the nickname "60-Minute Man" (football games last 60 minutes). He is in the Pro Football Hall of Fame as a center and as a linebacker.

Bednarik was part of two NFL championship teams with the Eagles (1949 and 1960). He played before the Super Bowl existed. Another of Bednarik's nicknames was "Concrete Charlie." It wasn't because of the way he played on the field. He was a concrete salesman during NFL offseasons.

"THE HIT"

In 1960, late in a game, the Philadelphia Eagles were tied at 10 with the New York Giants. New York was driving downfield. Running back Frank Gifford caught a pass. He was almost immediately hit with a clothesline tackle by Eagles linebacker Chuck Bednarik. The play, now known simply as "the hit," forced a fumble. The Eagles recovered it and returned for a touchdown. Gifford lay motionless on the field. A famous image seems to show Bednarik standing over Gifford in celebration. The hit was so hard that it forced Gifford to miss the entire 1961 season.

DICK BUTKUS

DICK BUTKUS (1942–2023)
LINEBACKER/CENTER
CHICAGO BEARS SEASONS: 1965–73
HALL OF FAME CLASS: 1979
AWARDS/HONORS: MEMBER OF NFL 75TH/100TH ANNIVERSARY TEAMS, 8X PRO BOWL, 8X ALL-PRO (5X FIRST TEAM), 1960S/1970S NFL ALL-DECADE TEAM, 2X NFL DEFENSIVE PLAYER OF THE YEAR

Dick Butkus played his entire football career in his home state. The Illinois native was born and raised in Chicago. He played college football at the University of Illinois. He was drafted by the Chicago Bears with the third selection in the 1965 NFL Draft. With the fourth selection, Chicago picked another future hall of famer in running back Gale Sayers. The Bears are the only team in NFL history to select future hall of famers with back-to-back selections.

Butkus was the most feared defensive player in the NFL in the 1960s and 1970s. He aced the middle linebacker position. In fact, he is known for being that position's "gold standard." His rookie year may have been his best. He set career highs with five interceptions and seven fumble recoveries. The recoveries are tied for third most by any NFL player in a season. Butkus holds the NFL record with 25 opponents' fumble recoveries in his career. He was skilled at moving sideline to sideline, delivering monster hits. He was a Pro Bowl selection in eight of his nine seasons. Butkus suffered a serious knee injury in 1970 that hampered the rest of his career.

After retiring, Butkus became an actor. He appeared in several movies, TV shows, and commercials. He also created the Butkus Foundation. The non-profit organization promotes health and wellness for people of all ages.

BOBBY BELL

BOBBY BELL (1940–)
LINEBACKER/DEFENSIVE END
KANSAS CITY CHIEFS SEASONS: 1963–74
HALL OF FAME CLASS: 1983
AWARDS/HONORS: MEMBER OF NFL 100TH ANNIVERSARY TEAM, 9X PRO BOWL, 7X ALL-PRO (6X FIRST TEAM), 1960S AMERICAN FOOTBALL LEAGUE (AFL) ALL-DECADE TEAM, SUPER BOWL CHAMPION, 2X AFL CHAMPION

Bobby Bell had an unusual path to becoming a Hall of Fame linebacker. In high school, Bell played quarterback. He started his football career at the University of Minnesota playing quarterback. He then transitioned to offensive lineman and defensive lineman. The Minnesota Vikings selected him in the second round of the 1963 NFL Draft. The Kansas City Chiefs, of the rival American Football League (AFL), waited until the seventh round to select Bell. He would choose to sign with the Chiefs.

Bell was strong in his first two pro seasons. He earned All-AFL honors playing defensive end. He switched to linebacker for his third season and continued to thrive. Bell intercepted 26 passes. He returned 6 for touchdowns over his 12-year pro career. He sacked the quarterback 40 times. Bell played in nine Pro Bowls. He was named First Team All-Pro six times. Chiefs' head coach Hank Stram once said, "He could play all 22 positions on the field and play them well."

Bell played for the Chiefs in the first Super Bowl, where they lost to the Green Bay Packers. The Chiefs returned following the 1969 season and defeated the Vikings, 23–7. Bell is the first Kansas City player to be inducted into the Pro Football Hall of Fame. More than 50 years after leaving college, Bell went back to the U of M to complete his degree.

JACK HAM

JACK HAM (1948–)
LINEBACKER
PITTSBURGH STEELERS SEASONS: 1971–82
HALL OF FAME CLASS: 1988
AWARDS/HONORS: MEMBER OF NFL 75TH/100TH ANNIVERSARY TEAMS, 8X PRO BOWL, 8X ALL-PRO (6X FIRST TEAM), 1970S ALL-DECADE TEAM, NFL DEFENSIVE PLAYER OF THE YEAR, 4X SUPER BOWL CHAMPION

Like Chuck Bednarik, Jack Ham played high school, college, and pro football in Pennsylvania. Raised in Johnstown, Ham played college ball at Penn State University. Penn State lost only three games during his three seasons as a starting linebacker. Ham was selected by the Pittsburgh Steelers in the second round of the 1971 NFL Draft.

Ham was a key figure in the famed "Steel Curtain" defense of the 1970s. From 1974 to 1979, Ham earned First Team All-Pro honors every season. The Steelers won four Super Bowls during that span. They were the "Team of the 1970s." Ham was skilled at sacking the quarterback and intercepting passes. Unofficially, he tallied 25.5 sacks over his 12-year career (sacks were not counted as official prior to 1982). Officially, he grabbed 32 interceptions. Those career interceptions are tied for third all time by a linebacker.

Ham rarely made mistakes and was seldom out of position. "I prefer to play consistent, error-free football," he said. "If you're doing your job well and defending your area, you might not get tested that often, or get a chance to make big plays." One of his biggest plays was in the 1974 American Football Conference (AFC) Championship Game against the Oakland Raiders. He had a 19-yard interception return. It set up a Steelers' go-ahead touchdown that led to them clinching their first Super Bowl appearance.

59
59
59
Steelers 50 Seasons

No. 58 Jack Lambert

LINEBACKER DUTIES

As their name suggests, linebackers play behind, or back up, the defensive line. They also play in front of the defensive backs. They can either rush the quarterback, tackle the running back, or drop back into pass coverage. Linebackers are usually the captains of the defense. In a defensive huddle, they are usually the ones calling the plays to their teammates. There are normally three or four linebackers on the field at a time. They are divided into middle and outside linebackers. Linebackers are often the ones that "blitz" the quarterback. During a blitz, more defenders than usual rush the passer.

JACK LAMBERT (1952–)
LINEBACKER
PITTSBURGH STEELERS SEASONS: 1974–84
HALL OF FAME CLASS: 1990
AWARDS/HONORS: MEMBER OF NFL 75TH/100TH ANNIVERSARY TEAMS, 9X PRO BOWL, 8X ALL-PRO (6X FIRST TEAM), 1970S/1980S ALL-DECADE TEAMS, NFL DEFENSIVE ROOKIE OF THE YEAR, NFL DEFENSIVE PLAYER OF THE YEAR, 4X SUPER BOWL CHAMPION

JACK LAMBERT

For nine seasons, Jack Ham was part of one of the best linebacker duos in NFL history. His partner was Pittsburgh Steelers teammate Jack Lambert. Coming from Kent State University, Lambert proved right away he was ready to be a pro football player. He was named NFL Defensive Rookie of the Year in 1974. Lambert was part of one of the greatest team draft classes in NFL history. He is one of four future Hall of Famers Pittsburgh selected in the 1974 NFL Draft. That season, the Steelers won the first of four Super Bowls in the 1970s.

Lambert continued to rule. He was named NFL Defensive Player of the Year in 1976, leading one of the best defenses of all time. Over the team's final 9 games that season, Pittsburgh allowed only 28 points. It shut out five opponents. Lambert's stellar resume includes nine straight Pro Bowl appearances and eight All-Pro mentions, including six First Team nods. Lambert displayed many of the qualities a linebacker needed. He had intelligence, drive, and quickness. He used those traits to amass 28 career interceptions and 23.5 career sacks (unofficially).

Lambert's name lives on in college football. Since 1991, the Jack Lambert Award is an award given every year to the season's best linebacker in college football.

TED HENDRICKS

TED HENDRICKS (1952–)
LINEBACKER
BALTIMORE COLTS SEASONS: 1969–73; GREEN BAY PACKERS SEASON: 1974; OAKLAND/LOS ANGELES RAIDERS SEASONS: 1975–83
HALL OF FAME CLASS: 1990
AWARDS/HONORS: MEMBER OF NFL 75TH/100TH ANNIVERSARY TEAMS, 8X PRO BOWL, 6X ALL-PRO (4X FIRST TEAM), 1970S/1980S ALL-DECADE TEAMS, GEORGE HALAS AWARD, 4X SUPER BOWL CHAMPION

He was nicknamed "The Mad Stork." He was tall, thin, and delivered brutal hits. Ted Hendricks was one of the greatest linebackers and special teams players in NFL history. Before his pro career, Hendricks was a defensive end star at the University of Miami. Because of his achievements, the Ted Hendricks Award was created. It honors the best college football defensive end each year. The Baltimore Colts drafted Hendricks in the second round of the 1969 AFL/NFL Draft. During Hendricks's rookie season, head coach Don Shula converted him into a linebacker. The rookie was a key member of the 1970 Colts defense that went on to win the Super Bowl.

After one year with the Green Bay Packers, Hendricks won three more Super Bowl titles with the Oakland/Los Angeles Raiders. He intercepted 26 passes over his 15-year career. He returned one for a touchdown. He unofficially recorded 61 quarterback sacks. Because of his height (6-foot-7), he was used a lot on special teams in hopes of blocking opponents' punts, field goals, and extra point attempts. He did so 25 times in his career. Hendricks is tied for an NFL record of recording four safeties. That's where an opposing team's ball carrier is tackled in his own end zone.

Outside of football, the Ted Hendricks Foundation supports health, recreational, and educational programs for youths and seniors. A native of Guatemala, Hendricks was awarded the Order of the Quetzal, which is the country's highest civilian honor.

MIKE SINGLETARY

MIKE SINGLETARY (1958–)
LINEBACKER
CHICAGO BEARS SEASONS: 1981–92
HALL OF FAME CLASS: 1998
AWARDS/HONORS: 10X PRO BOWL, 8X ALL-PRO (7X FIRST TEAM), 1980S NFL ALL-DECADE TEAM, NFL MAN OF THE YEAR, 2X NFL DEFENSIVE PLAYER OF THE YEAR, SUPER BOWL CHAMPION

The 1985 Chicago Bears defense is considered one of the best units in NFL history. They were known as "The Monsters of the Midway." Chicago finished with a 15–1 record. They shut out both teams they faced in the National Football Conference (NFC) playoffs. And they routed the New England Patriots in Super Bowl XX (20), 46–10. The leader of the defense was linebacker Mike Singletary. He was extremely intimidating. Singletary was named NFL Defensive Player of the Year that season. He earned the honor again in 1988.

Singletary ruled, despite his small size. His 6-foot height is considered small for a linebacker. But lack of height didn't stop him from looking for that big hit. "Hitting people has always been my style," he said. "I'm not tall but sometimes small things are the most dangerous. It's like a snake when it's coiled. You don't know when it'll strike, and whoosh, it's got you." Singletary used that snake-like mentality to make 10-straight Pro Bowls. He also earned eight All-Pro honors, including seven First Team All-Pro nods.

Singletary earned honors off the field as well. In 1990, he earned the NFL's highest honor—NFL Man of the Year. The award is presented annually to honor a player's impact on the community. It was later named for Singletary's former teammate Walter Payton.

LAWRENCE TAYLOR

LAWRENCE TAYLOR (1959–)
LINEBACKER
NEW YORK GIANTS SEASONS: 1981–93
HALL OF FAME CLASS: 1999
AWARDS/HONORS: MEMBER OF NFL 75TH/100TH ANNIVERSARY TEAMS, 10X PRO BOWL, 10X ALL-PRO (8X FIRST TEAM), 1980S NFL ALL-DECADE TEAM, NFL MOST VALUABLE PLAYER, 3X NFL DEFENSIVE PLAYER OF THE YEAR, NFL DEFENSIVE ROOKIE OF THE YEAR, 2X SUPER BOWL CHAMPION

Only two defensive players in history have been named NFL Most Valuable Player. One is Alan Page of the Minnesota Vikings. The other is New York Giants' linebacker Lawrence Taylor. Taylor was the second overall pick in the 1981 NFL Draft by the Giants. He went on to have one of the most impactful rookie seasons ever. In 1980, New York's defense allowed the second most points in the league. With Taylor's addition the following year, New York allowed the third fewest points. The Giants qualified for the playoffs for the first time in 18 years. Taylor was named NFL Defensive Rookie of the Year and NFL Defensive Player of the Year. That's the only time in history that has happened.

Taylor's best season was 1986. The Giants went 14–2. Taylor led the NFL with a career high total of 20.5 sacks. He was named NFL Defensive Player of the Year and NFL MVP. The Giants cruised through the playoffs en route to their first Super Bowl championship. Taylor helped the Giants to another Super Bowl title after the 1990 season.

Taylor earned All-Pro honors in each of his first 10 seasons in the league. Eight times he received First Team All-Pro nods. In addition to his MVP honor, he won three NFL Defensive Player of the Year awards. He recorded 132.5 career sacks (not counting the 9.5 in 1981, as sacks were not official until 1982).

DERRICK THOMAS

DERRICK THOMAS (1967–2000)
LINEBACKER
KANSAS CITY CHIEFS SEASONS: 1989–99
HALL OF FAME CLASS: 2009
AWARDS/HONORS: 9X PRO BOWL, 5X ALL-PRO (2X FIRST TEAM), 1990S NFL ALL-DECADE TEAM, NFL MAN OF THE YEAR

One of the greatest pass-rushing linebackers of all time was Derrick Thomas. Thomas had a stellar college ball career at the University of Alabama. He was then selected fourth overall in the 1989 NFL Draft by the Kansas City Chiefs. He collected 10 sacks, 75 tackles, and forced 3 fumbles on his way to Defensive Rookie of the Year honors. He also was named to the first of nine straight Pro Bowls. Thomas recorded double-digit sacks in each of his first four seasons.

Thomas did even better in his second season. He led the league with 20 sacks and 6 forced fumbles. In a November 1990 game, Thomas sacked Seattle Seahawks' quarterback Dave Krieg seven times. That still stands as an NFL single-game record. Thomas nearly equaled that in 1998. In a game against the Oakland Raiders, Thomas sacked quarterback Jeff George six times. He also got a safety. Thomas finished his 11-year career with 126.5 sacks.

Thomas was a hero in the community, too. He formed the Derrick Thomas Third and Long Foundation. It focuses on illiteracy and bettering the lives of urban children in critical situations. Tragically, Thomas died shortly after the 1999 season following complications from an auto accident.

DERRICK BROOKS

DERRICK BROOKS (1973–)
LINEBACKER
TAMPA BAY BUCCANEERS SEASONS: 1995–2008
HALL OF FAME CLASS: 2014
AWARDS/HONORS: MEMBER OF NFL 100TH ANNIVERSARY TEAM, 11X PRO BOWL, 9X ALL-PRO (5X FIRST TEAM), 2000S NFL ALL-DECADE TEAM, NFL DEFENSIVE PLAYER OF THE YEAR, NFL MAN OF THE YEAR, SUPER BOWL CHAMPION

Another Hall of Fame linebacker who played all of his football in one state was Derrick Brooks. A native of Pensacola, Florida, Brooks played at Florida State University, where he won a national championship. He was drafted by the Tampa Bay Buccaneers in the first round of the 1995 NFL Draft. When he got to Tampa, the team was not very good. Its last winning season was 1982. By Brooks's third season, Tampa Bay was in the playoffs. The charge was led by Brooks and the stellar defense. Tampa Bay reached the top in 2002, winning Super Bowl XXXVII (37). Brooks was named NFL Defensive Player of the Year.

Brooks never missed a game during his 14-year career. He started every game but three in his rookie season. With Brooks as the anchor, Tampa Bay's defense led the NFL in total defense twice and led the NFC five times. Brooks led the league in solo tackles three times and in combined tackles once. He earned a Pro Bowl trip in 11 of his 14 seasons in the league. He was on nine All-Pro teams, five of which were First Team nods. By the time he retired in 2008, Brooks held 11 team regular season records and 3 postseason records.

Brooks is well known for his charity work. He won the NFL Man of the Year award in 2000. He is the founder of Derrick Brooks Charities. The charity runs a "mobile classroom" that takes local youths across the United States and South Africa.

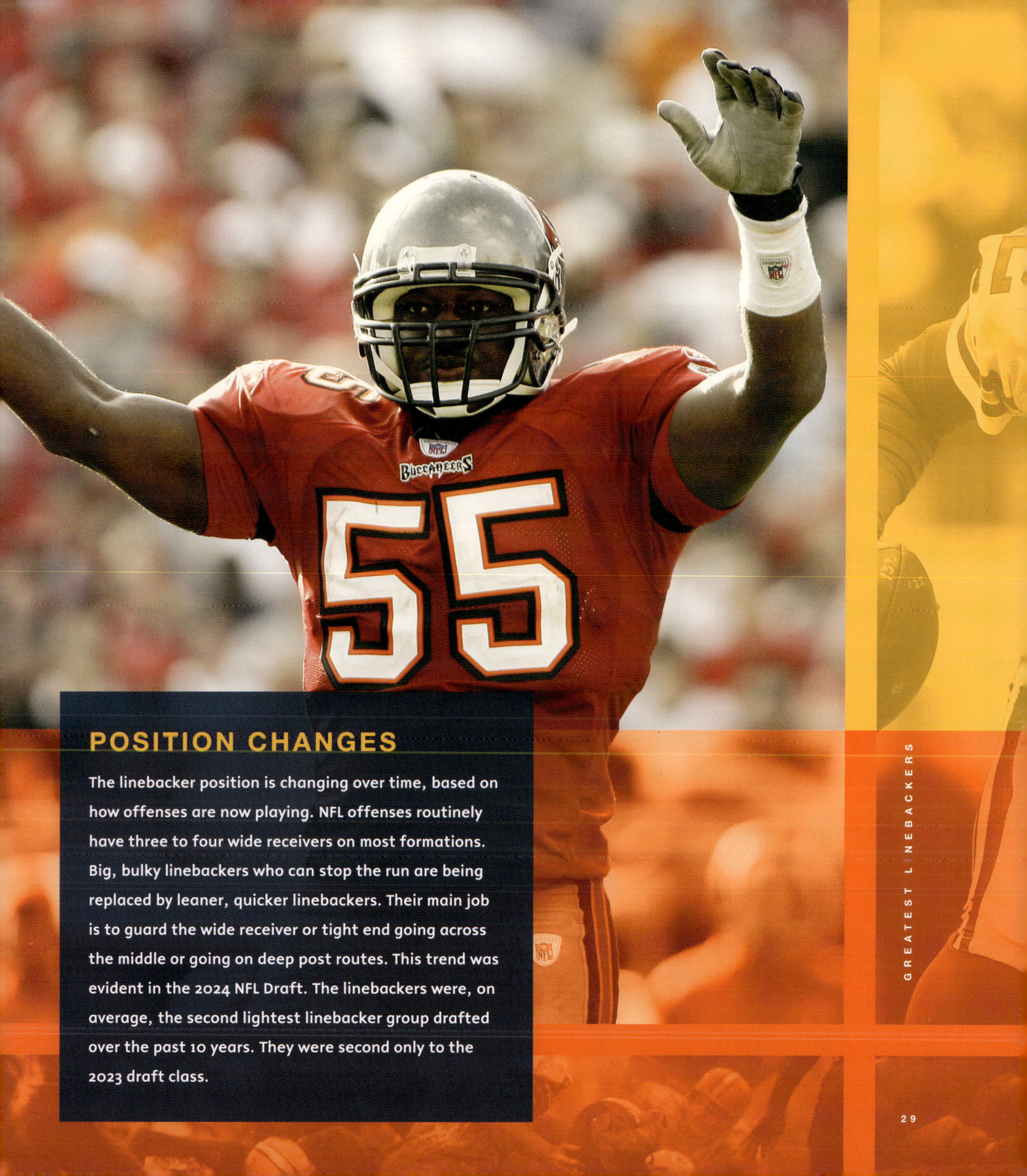

POSITION CHANGES

The linebacker position is changing over time, based on how offenses are now playing. NFL offenses routinely have three to four wide receivers on most formations. Big, bulky linebackers who can stop the run are being replaced by leaner, quicker linebackers. Their main job is to guard the wide receiver or tight end going across the middle or going on deep post routes. This trend was evident in the 2024 NFL Draft. The linebackers were, on average, the second lightest linebacker group drafted over the past 10 years. They were second only to the 2023 draft class.

21
21
52

RAY LEWIS

RAY LEWIS (1975–)
LINEBACKER
BALTIMORE RAVENS SEASONS: 1996–2012
HALL OF FAME CLASS: 2018
AWARDS/HONORS: MEMBER OF NFL 100TH ANNIVERSARY TEAM, 13X PRO BOWL, 10X ALL-PRO (7X FIRST TEAM), 2000S NFL ALL-DECADE TEAM, 2X NFL DEFENSIVE PLAYER OF THE YEAR, 2X SUPER BOWL CHAMPION, SUPER BOWL MVP

The Baltimore Ravens' first draft as an NFL franchise was one to remember. With the fourth overall pick, Baltimore chose offensive lineman Jonathan Ogden. He would later be elected to the Pro Football Hall of Fame. Later in the first round, the Ravens selected linebacker Ray Lewis. He, too, would make the Hall of Fame. By 2000, the duo would help bring the franchise their first Super Bowl championship. Lewis was the leader of the 2000 Ravens defense. The unit would be one of the most feared and powerful defenses in NFL history. Baltimore set league records for fewest points allowed in a 16-game regular season and fewest rushing yards allowed. The team recorded four shutouts. Lewis was named MVP of Super Bowl XXXV (35) as the Ravens destroyed the New York Giants, 34–7. The Giants' only points of the game were on a kickoff return for a touchdown.

Lewis was also named NFL Defensive Player of the Year for the 2000 season. It's an honor he would again receive following the 2003 season. Three times in his career, he led the NFL in both combined and solo tackles. Twelve times in his 17-year career, he was named to the Pro Bowl. Ten times he earned All-Pro honors, seven of those times were First Team mentions.

In 2012, Lewis suffered a major arm injury midway through the season but returned in time for the playoffs. He led the team to four postseason wins, which included another Super Bowl championship.

INDEX